22 March – 28 April 1995

Celia Paul
Paintings & Drawings

Marlborough Fine Art (London) Ltd
6 Albemarle Street, London W1X 4BY
Telephone: 0171-629 5161
Telefax: 0171-629 6338

Photograph: Rose Boyt

CELIA PAUL

The experience of sitting for Celia has changed for me over the
years. As a schoolgirl, and then an undergraduate, I would agree to
sit only if allowed to read a book at the same time - at least until the
moment when Celia had to paint my hands. It is only subsequently
that I have realised what a hard bargain this was for Celia: she
wanted active participation; a subject, not an object. There is a very
early painting of me with my mother and father. I am obviously
trying to concentrate on my Anglo-Saxon primer; my father is
doggedly sitting it out for another ten minutes before getting back
to his sermon; only my mother leaps out of the canvas, like a living
creature in a still life. In fact, I find the lack of engagement with
my father and me gives a stillness and a coldness that is very
powerful, but only because it is broken by my mother's energy: that
fiercely protective maternal stare. Looking at this picture again
now, it is as if this figure of my mother was reaching out to become
a bridge to Celia's later work. Nowadays, there is always a complete
engagement with the sitter - one of the reasons why Celia only
paints people she knows well. Intimacy gives her freedom to
express a wider vision, whilst remaining firmly rooted in her
knowledge of the people she paints; in the case of group paintings,
like the recent one of me with my mother and my sister Jane, in our
relationship with each other, and with Celia herself. But it is never
contrived or staged. As often as not, I find a position for myself,
rather than being placed by Celia. She does not make up a story, and
expect her sitters to fill the roles. She watches to see what we do,
how we look, what we are feeling: that will be the story. And it will
not just be about a moment in my life, or the life of my mother, or
one of Celia's friends; increasingly, her figures appear to inhabit a
larger world, an eternal and monumental landscape.

Kate Paul
February 1995

CATALOGUE

Oil paintings on canvas

1
Family Group 1979
59 ½ × 50 in. / 151.1 × 127 cm.

2
My Mother - Great Russell Street 1992
66 ¼ × 66 ¼ in. / 168.2 × 168.2 cm.
Private Collection

3
Gillian I 1991-92
30 × 24 in. / 76.2 × 61 cm.
Private Collection

4
Linda and Margot 1992
42 × 40 in. / 106.7 × 101.6 cm.
Private Collection

5
Kate 1993-95
58 × 50 in. / 147.3 × 127 cm.

6
Head of Mandy 1991
14⅛ × 14 in. / 35.9 × 35.6 cm.
Private Collection.

7
Portrait of Sarah 1993
14 × 10 in. / 35.6 × 25.4 cm.
Private Collection

8
My Mother at Icklingham 1992
64 1/16 × 62 in. / 162.7 × 157.5 cm.

9
My Mother - Head in Hands 1993
58 ¼ × 60 ¼ in. / 148 × 153 cm.
Private Collection

10
Kate (on ripped sofa) 1992
60 $\frac{1}{8}$ × 54 $\frac{1}{8}$ in. / 157.7 × 137.5 cm.
Private Collection

11
Study for Gillian Seated 1993-94
12 × 10 in. / 30.5 × 25.4 cm.
Private Collection

12
My Mother smiling 1988
11 $\frac{1}{4}$ × 9 $\frac{3}{4}$ in. / 28.5 × 25 cm.
Private Collection

13
Head of Kate 1993-94
17 × 11 in. / 43.1 × 28 cm.

14
Profile Portrait 1993-94
54 $\frac{1}{8}$ × 36 in. / 137.5 × 91.5 cm.

15
Three Women 1994
65 $\frac{1}{4}$ × 70 $\frac{1}{8}$ in. / 165.4 × 178.1 cm.

16
Gillian II 1994-95
48 × 48 in. / 122 × 122 cm.

17
Steve 1994-95
16 × 12 in. / 41 × 30.5 cm.

Works on Paper

18
My Mother 1993-94
16 $\frac{1}{8}$ × 16 $\frac{1}{2}$ in. / 40.9 × 41.9 cm.
ink and pastel on paper
Photograph courtesy of the Trustees of the British Museum

19
My Mother 1994-95
30 $\frac{1}{2}$ × 22 in. / 77.5 × 55.9 cm.
ink and pastel on paper

20
Kate 1995
20 $\frac{1}{4}$ × 20 in. / 51.5 × 51 cm.
ink and pastel on paper

21
My Mother Lying Down (work in progress)
58 × 60 in. / 147.3 × 152.4 cm.

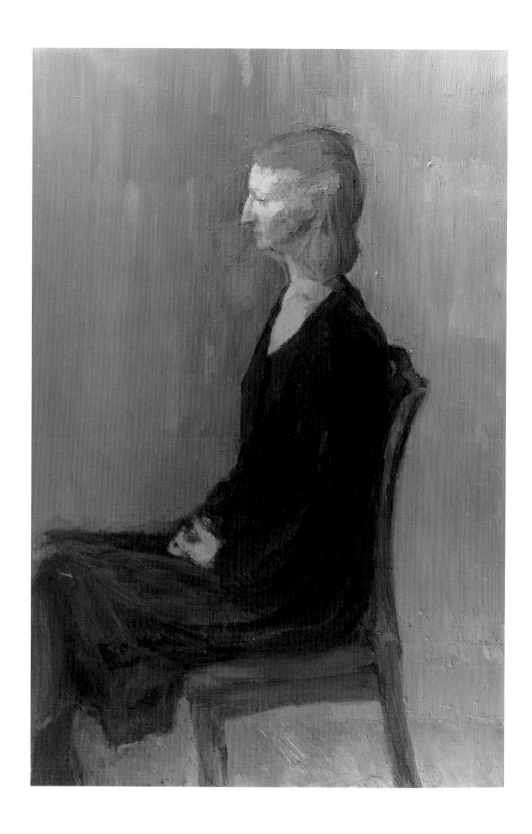

CELIA PAUL

Biography

1959	Born in Trivandrum, India
1976-1981	Slade School of Art, London
	Lives and works in London

One-Woman Exhibitions:

1986	Bernard Jacobson Gallery, London
1991	Marlborough Fine Art, London
	Marlborough Graphics, London

Group Exhibitions:

1989	'The School of London: Works on Paper', Odette Gilbert Gallery, London
1991	'The Marlborough Gallery Re-Opening Exhibition', Marlborough Fine Art, London
1994	Contemporary Art Society Market, Royal Festival Hall, 1-6 November
1995	Art '95, Marlborough Fine Art at the London Contemporary Art Fair, Business Design Centre, London, 18-22nd January
	Art '95, The Museum of Women's Art exhibition (in conjunction with Harpers & Queen), Business Design Centre, London, 18-22nd January

Bibliography:

Sarah Kent, 'Celia Paul (Bernard Jacobson)', *Time Out*,
17-23 September 1986
William Feaver, 'Making it in Britain', *The Observer*,
21 September 1986
Alistair Hicks, 'The School of London - the resurgence of
contemporary painting', *Phaidon Press Ltd.*, Oxford, 1989
Martin Golding, 'Celia Paul', *Modern Painters*, vol. 4, no.2,
Autumn 1991
Alistair Hicks, 'Women and God', *Antique*, vol. 6, no.3,
Autumn 1991
Giles Auty, 'Sixties Secessionists', *The Spectator*, 28 September 1991
Christine Rodenbeck, 'Celia Paul', *Countryweek*, 3 October 1991
Ralph Sagar, 'Celia Paul, Marlborough Galleries', *What's On*,
9 October 1991
Matthew Collings, *City Limits*, 10-17 October 1991
William Packer, *Financial Times*, 15 October 1991
Vogue, Christmas 1993

Public Collections:

British Museum, London
Fitzwilliam Museum, Cambridge
Metropolitan Museum, New York
Saatchi Collection, London

MARLBOROUGH

LONDON

Marlborough Fine Art (London) Ltd
6 Albemarle Street
London W1X 4BY
Telephone: 0171-629 5161
Telefax: 0171-629 6338

NEW YORK

Marlborough Gallery, Inc.
40 West 57th Street
New York, NY 10019
Telephone: 1-212-541 4900
Telefax: 1-212-541 4948

TOKYO

Marlborough Fine Art Ltd. Tokyo
Ginza AH Building 4th Floor
3-5, Ginza 4-chome
Chuo-ku
Tokyo 104
Telephone: 81-3-3563 5884
Telefax: 81-3-3563 5872

MADRID

Galeria Marlborough, S A.
Orfila 5
28010 Madrid
Telephone: 34-1-319 1414
Telefax: 34-1-308 4345

Catalogue no. 476
ISBN 0 900955 503

Designed by Derek Birdsall and
produced by Omnific Studios/London
Printed in England by
Balding+Mansell

© 1995 Marlborough

LONDON

Agents for

Frank Auerbach
Christopher Bramham
Steven Campbell
Lynn Chadwick
Stephen Conroy
Christopher Couch
John Davies
Dieter Hacker
Bill Jacklin
Ken Kiff
R.B. Kitaj
Christopher Le Brun
Raymond Mason
Thérèse Oulton
Victor Pasmore
Celia Paul
John Piper
Paula Rego
The Estate of Francis Bacon
The Estate of Barbara Hepworth
The Estate of Oskar Kokoschka
The Estate of Kurt Schwitters
The Estate of Graham Sutherland

IMPORTANT WORKS AVAILABLE BY
Impressionists and Post-Impressionists
Twentieth Century European Masters
German Expressionists
Post War American Artists

Modern Masters and
Contemporary Graphics
available from
Marlborough Graphics Ltd.

Photographic Credits:
Prudence Cuming Associates
Rose Boyt

NEW YORK

Agents for

Magdalena Abakanowicz
John Alexander
Avigdor Arikha
Fernando Botero
Claudio Bravo
Grisha Bruskin
Vincent Desiderio
Richard Estes
Red Grooms
Israel Hershberg
Alex Katz
Marisol
Arnaldo Pomodoro
Larry Rivers
Altoon Sultan
James Surls
Neil Welliver
The Estate of Jacques Lipchitz
The Estate of James Rosati

MADRID

Agents for

Juan Genovés
Luis Gordillo
Francisco Leiro
Antonio López Garcia
Lucio Muñoz
Daniel Quintero
Joaquín Ramo
Manolo Valdés